Contents

When you enter a mindset, you enter a new world. In one world – the world of fixed traits – success is about proving you're smart or talented. Validating yourself. In the other – the world of changing qualities – it's about stretching yourself to learn something new. Developing yourself.

Dweck (2007), p. 14

Introduction

There isn't a direct link between success at the end of Year 11 and success at college.

You might think that those students who succeed at the end of Year 11 continue this pathway and succeed again at the end of their college course. But instead something else happens: some students make giant strides between 16 and 18, leaping up from pretty modest results in Year 11 to outstanding results in college. Others go from great performance at 16 to modest grades at the end of their college courses. Some students hit ceilings, others make sudden breakthroughs.

We've spent years studying what it is about 'ceiling students' that stops them progressing, and what it is about 'breakthrough students' that makes them suddenly improve. Here's the outcome: there isn't a link between GCSE performance and being a breakthrough student or, indeed, a ceiling student. *Past performance doesn't guarantee future performance.* Whatever happened to you in your GCSEs doesn't define what you'll achieve now.

Instead, the factors which determine students' further education success are their habits, routines, attitudes and approaches to study. Paul Tough summarises it pretty neatly in the following observation. It is your behaviours, not your intelligence, that will determine your results:

'Economists refer to these as non-cognitive skills, psychologists call them personality traits, and the rest of us sometimes think of them as character' (Tough, 2013, p. 5).

VESPA

Our work suggests that students who are successful score highly in the following characteristics or qualities:

» **VISION** – they know what they want to achieve.

» **EFFORT** – they put in many hours of proactive independent study.

» **SYSTEMS** – they organise their learning resources and their time.

» **PRACTICE** – they practise and develop their skills.

» **ATTITUDE** – they respond constructively to setbacks.

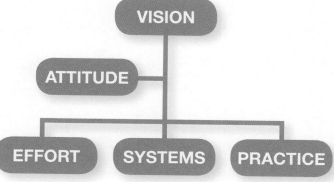

These characteristics beat cognition hands down. We've found that ceiling students have significant gaps in one or more of these characteristics. And regardless of their academic success at 16, our studies show that these learners will hit the ceiling at college if they don't address and strengthen those weaknesses. Conversely, students who score highly for the qualities above can and do make significant breakthroughs at college, unlocking performance that far outstrips their target grades.

> **Students who are success seekers are not bluffed by setback, poor performance, failure or academic adversity. They take the lesson to be learnt and move on.** Martin (2010), p. 22

The VESPA Activities

The activities in this booklet are designed to:

» Raise awareness about the impact a quality/ characteristic can have on your potential success.

» Encourage you to reflect on the strength of that quality on a personal level.

» Engage you in a task that develops you as a learner – a reflection, discussion, coaching conversation or experiment.

Each session is designed to take fifteen to twenty minutes to complete. We've included eight tasks under each heading, giving you a total of forty to start experimenting with.

Good luck!

1. Vision

Vision

1. Vision Activity: Twenty Questions

It turns out that asking, 'What is your goal?' isn't a very good way of unlocking your vision. The question is abstract and slippery and answering it is often embarrassing and frightening. But there are questions that work. Some questions get an immediate response, 'Ah! I know the answer to that!' where others don't. The following questions have been tested over and over again with students and seem to be ones that are more likely to open up some positive thinking.

We can't promise these questions will work for you; all we know is that they've worked for others. Answer these questions with reference to study and work. Try your best to answer without feeling stupid or embarrassed, and to say what you feel and think. Try to write all your answers down – it really helps!

» If you could only take one subject what would it be, and why?

....

» What lessons or elements of study do you find easy?

....

» What do you do with your spare time?

....

» Describe an interesting lesson you had recently. Why was it interesting?

....

....

....

» What jobs do you avoid doing, and why?

....

....

» When does time fly? What are you doing?

....

....

» When does time seem to drag or stop? What are you doing?

....

....

» What job would you do for free?

....

» Who do you look up to?

....

» What would you try if you knew you couldn't fail?

....

....

» What puts a smile on your face?

....

» If you had the afternoon off to work at home, which piece of work would you choose to do?

....

» When you have a lot of assignments, which subject do you do first?

....

» Describe an assignment you have recently left until the last minute or not done at all. Why?

....

....

» What do you get obsessed about?

....

....

....

» When you're with your friends, what do you want to talk about?

....

....

» What stresses you out?

....

Vision

» If you had a laptop and an hour off college work, what would you type into a search engine?

. . . .

. . . .

» If you were given a small amount of money to start a company, what would it be?

. . . .

. . . .

. . . .

» List five words you associate with 'happiness'.

. . . .

. . . .

. . . .

. . . .

. . . .

Now scan over your answers to look for patterns. A good way to do this is to record the information in a table like this one:

'Interests and passions' Use this column to record your positive responses – things you know you enjoy, love or look forward to	'Dislikes' Use this column to record your negative responses – things you avoid or find uninteresting or dull

Final Thoughts

» Can you see themes and patterns developing?

» Are there interests and passions emerging that are clear and positive?

» Could you attach a job, course or career to these passions?

Use the space below to record your observations and plans:

. . . .

. . . .

. . . .

. . . .

. . . .

. . . .

. . . .

. . . .

. . . .

. . . .

2. Vision Activity: Getting Dreams Done

There is a big difference between a dream and a goal. A dream is something you imagine happening; a goal is something you take actions towards. Often, when we meet with students to discuss their vision they list their dreams, not their goals. Here is a good way of distinguishing between them.

Make a list of your hopes for the future and then put them into one of the following categories:

Pure fantasy and pipe dreams List here the things you would one day like to be or do but that you've never ever talked about. It's never been verbalised at all – it's just in your head.	....
Daydreams and conversations List here the things you would one day like to be or do that you've talked about with a friend. You've admitted them and started exploring and discussing them.	....
Goals List here the things you would like to do that you've taken action about. What was the action? When did you take it? What did you do when things got difficult?	....

When your list is complete, answer the following questions:

1 What percentage of your daydreams or pipe dreams have you acted on? What is the chance of these hopes becoming reality?

....

....

....

....

2 How much action have you taken to turn daydreams into reality? Has it been repeated, determined action? Or has it been action taken some time ago?

....

....

....

....

3 Which daydreams are the most important to you? What further actions could you take? What could you do to turn pure fantasy and pipe dreams into goals?

....

....

....

....

Final Thoughts

Most people have pipe dreams or daydreams they never act on. That's OK, as long as you aren't frustrated or unhappy by not pursuing your dreams. Look over your three lists again, and try to answer this question honestly:

If you could turn one of these dreams into reality, which one would it be, and what would you have to do?

....

....

....

....

3. Vision Activity: Your 21st Birthday

Imagine it's your 21st birthday. You need to picture an unusual 21st at which your family and friends stand up and describe the type of person that you are for them.

Answer the following questions:

» What would you like your friends to say about you?

. . . .

. . . .

. . . .

» What qualities would you like them to admire in you?

. . . .

. . . .

. . . .

» How would you like to be described by your colleagues?

. . . .

. . . .

. . . .

» When they list your achievements so far, what do you want them to be?

. . . .

. . . .

. . . .

» When they describe all the things you are still going to do, and the hopes they have for your future, what will they say?

. . . .

. . . .

. . . .

By creating a vision of what you would like to be in the near future, in different areas of your life, you often reflect the personal values that are most important to you in each of these different areas. Write down what you would like each person to say about you – your qualities, characteristics and achievements – in the following areas:

Professionally (things you have achieved in your work):

. . . .

. . . .

. . . .

. . . .

Socially (relationships you have with family and friends):

. . . .

. . . .

. . . .

. . . .

Personally (qualities you have as an individual):

. . . .

. . . .

. . . .

. . . .

Final Thoughts

If you could pick one of the above that you feel you're on track to make happen by the age of 21, which would it be?

. . . .

What about one of the above that you feel furthest away from achieving by the age of 21? And what can you do to accelerate your progress here?

. . . .

. . . .

. . . .

4. Vision Activity: Fix Your Dashboard

Imagine somebody that you admire and respect. Take your time and choose someone you look up to – often, your first thought isn't your best. Perhaps list five or ten people you admire to begin with and see what they have in common:

....

....

....

....

....

....

....

....

....

What qualities do they have that you admire? The characteristics that you admire in others can say a lot about the type of person that you would like to be:

....

....

....

....

....

Now write down the qualities of this person in each life domain: career, finance, family, personal relationships, education, characteristics, activities, community citizenship and any others that you can think of:

....

....

....

....

....

....

. . . .

. . . .

. . . .

Next, write a paragraph on the type of person that *you* would like to be in each area of your life. Practise 'no limit' thinking. Don't limit yourself by your fears, lack of money or a lack of time – clarify a vision of your ideal self:

. . . .

. . . .

. . . .

. . . .

. . . .

. . . .

. . . .

. . . .

. . . .

The Dashboard

Millions of people drive to work every day. The dashboard of their car is the first thing they see on the way in and the last thing they see as they arrive home. We use the word 'dashboard' to mean what you see first thing in the morning or last thing at night. It might be the wall above your desk or next to your bedside table. It might be the wallpaper on your phone or the inside cover of your files.

We each live with a mental dashboard of people and ideas. Our research shows us that people who have even a brief reminder of a positive role model – from looking at their dashboard – have hugely increased levels of motivation.

We have also worked with students who have altered their dashboards:

» One student put a photograph of the university she wanted to go to inside her file, so she saw it each time she opened it up to work.

» Another student covered his bedroom wall with inspiring quotes and messages.

» Another listed all the people who would feel proud and excited if she did really well, and stared at those names before each revision session.

What kind of images and quotes will you be including in your dashboard?

. . . .

. . . .

. . . .

. . . .

. . . .

. . . .

. . . .

. . . .

. . . .

. . . .

Final Thoughts

For further information on this, check out Dan Coyle's brilliant guide, *The Little Book of Talent* (2012), which encourages people to study the person you want to become.

5. Vision Activity: The Perfect Day

Every primary school child in the country will be able to tell you what they want to be. Why? Because at that age teachers encourage children to express their hopes and dreams in writing activities with titles like, 'When I grow up …' Look in your old school books and you will find you've done this too.

But no one asks teenagers to write about what they want to be. It's as if, by this age, we're embarrassed to have hopes and dreams. We shouldn't be. *Having hopes and dreams is more important at this age than at any other time of life.*

So, put your headphones in, get some music on and write without shame. Here are some questions to help get you thinking. Your task is to have a go at describing your perfect day at work to help you develop a long-term vision.

» Are you working indoors or outdoors?

. . . .

. . . .

» Do you work at home or away from home?

. . . .

. . . .

» Who are you with?

. . . .

. . . .

» Are you leading a team? Part of a team? Alone?

. . . .

. . . .

» When do you start or finish your day?

. . . .

. . . .

» What are you wearing to work?

. . . .

. . . .

» What is your workspace like?

. . . .

. . . .

Your answers to these questions might not tell you precisely what kind of job you should be aiming for, but they will help establish what interesting work looks like for you. Look over your answers.

If you had to pick one of the above as a non-negotiable – in other words, something you would need in your work to be truly happy – which one would it be?

. . . .

Final Thoughts

We've found the following topics tend to emerge as important factors in student responses. Do any apply to you? Ideas about travel, being outdoors, working in teams, celebrating successes, helping others, playing challenging games, creating fictional worlds, responding artistically to something, exercise and physical activity, companionship and leadership.

. . . .

. . . .

. . . .

6. Vision Activity: SMART Goals

In this goal setting activity you are going to develop SMART goals – that is, something concrete and doable which will help you reach your goal. SMART goals are a proven method of maximising goal setting success.

Pick one of your goals. Whether you choose an education goal, a career goal or a personal goal, try to identify how you can make your goal SMART:

» **Specific.** Be as precise as you can rather than general.

» **Measurable.** How will you know when you've reached your goal? Write: 'I will know I have achieved my goal because …'

» **Action-based.** What can you do to get the goal started? How? What's step one, step two, step three and so on?

» **Realistic.** Has someone done it before? Could you speak to that person? Is there evidence to suggest that you can do it? What previous personal successes are connected to your goal?

» **Time-bound.** When do you want to do this by? Avoid, 'One day I'm going to …'; instead be much more precise.

Use the template below to record one long-term SMART goal, like a university course or a dream job:

Specific	
Measurable	
Action-based	
Realistic	
Time-bound	

Short-Term SMARTs

SMART goals take your goal setting to the next level, but they need practice. Try setting four or five SMART goals for the next fortnight using the same grid, below. Imagine how you would feel if you had every one of those five short-term goals done in the next ten working days! You might want to choose one per subject – for example:

» An assignment you want to complete really well.

» A part-time job application and interview you want to go smoothly.

» An upcoming test you want to perform well in.

» A section of notes you want to reorganise and revise.

Specific	
Measurable	
Action-based	
Realistic	
Time-bound	

Final Thoughts

Could you use the SMART goal setting technique to create a goal for each of your subjects?
You would need to be clear on the grade you wanted, how you were going to prepare for the exams, what resources you intend to use, when you will have mastered sections of the syllabus by and precisely when the exams were!

7. Vision Activity: Mental Contrasting

This is a positive thinking exercise that helps you define your vision. In her book, *Rethinking Positive Thinking* (2014), Gabrielle Oettingen argues that too much positive visualisation can rob a person of their desire to succeed – they get happy enough just dreaming about something and never end up doing it. Any goal you set will usually have obstacles in the way of you achieving them (if they were easy everyone would be able to achieve them!).

Mental contrasting gets you to think about these obstacles and develop an 'if … then' plan to help you overcome them. The process also gets you thinking about the feasibility of your goals. If you can't formulate an 'if … then' plan, then your goal might not be possible at all!

Use the grid on the next page to record your thoughts and ideas:

1. WISH

Spend a minute or two thinking in detail about something you want to accomplish. (For example, this could be the grade you want to achieve in a particular subject.)

2. OUTCOME

Vividly imagine the best thing you associate with having achieved that outcome. (That 'best thing' might be anything related to the outcome. It might mean getting into the university of your dreams!)

3. OBSTACLE

Ask yourself what internal obstacles are most likely to get in the way. (That weakness inside you that holds you back from higher grades or a better exam performance.)

4. PLAN

Formulate an if … then plan for what you will do when that obstacle arises. ('If I find myself checking Twitter, Facebook or going on Netflix, I'll get up immediately and turn off the Wi-Fi.')

Vision

1. Wish	2. Outcome
. . . .	. . . .
. . . .	. . . .
. . . .	. . . .
. . . .	. . . .
. . . .	. . . .

3. Obstacle	4. Plan
. . . .	. . . .
. . . .	. . . .
. . . .	. . . .
. . . .	. . . .
. . . .	. . . .

Final Thoughts

Creating a vision this way allows you to record and recognise the elements of your own personality that are likely to prevent you from reaching your goals.

What do you consider to be one of your most significant weaknesses?

. . . .

. . . .

How might you overcome it?

. . . .

. . . .

8. Vision Activity: Fake It

Sometimes it feels almost impossible to make a decision. We've worked with lots of students who are torn between two or more goals. They can't decide between the two, three or even four options they've got. If this is the case for you, we have a solution – the 'fake it' method.

Here's how it works:

Week 1

Choose one of your options. It might be applying to university to study criminology, getting an apprenticeship or starting your own business.

For a whole week, you're going to pretend that you've made your decision; that the option you've chosen for the week is what you want to do with your life more than anything else. The burden of having to make a decision is gone – you've made the decision. You're not allowed to think about the other options at all for the whole week.

In pretending you've already made your decision, do the following:

» Research the option – find out all you can about it. Use the section in the table below called 'the facts' to record your discoveries.

» Get excited about the positives. What's on the course? How much will you earn on this apprenticeship? What are the career prospects afterwards? Who else among the people you know has chosen that option? Why are they choosing it? What is making them excited? Use 'the positives' section of the table (on page 26) to collect your findings.

Option 1, week 1	Option 2, week 2
The facts:	The facts:

Option 1, week 1	Option 2, week 2
The positives:	The positives:

On Friday, make a note of the way the week has made you feel. Has it been a good week? Discuss it with a friend or a tutor and record some of your thoughts here:

....

....

....

....

....

Week 2

Choose another one of your options. (Not the week one option – you're ditching that.) Now, you're going to pretend that this is your decision. Repeat the process above, using the same table so you can see your notes side by side.

Now compare and contrast:

» Which was the better week?

» Which made you feel more excited?

» Which was more enjoyable?

» Which felt more like you?

Spend time with a tutor or friend explaining your responses. Use the space below to record your impressions:

. . . .

. . . .

. . . .

. . . .

. . . .

Final Thoughts

We've encouraged students to use the 'fake it' technique to make decisions about other things too. Think about how you might use it to choose between employers, gap year options, a choice of coursework tasks, or university courses and accommodation choices.

A Vision Journal

The eight activities in this section have all been encouraging you to think about what matters to you, what makes you happy, what you want to achieve, and how you might plan for avoiding pitfalls and problems. Use this space to record your learning!

. . . .

. . . .

. . . .

. . . .

. . . .

. . . .

. . . .

. . . .

. . . .

. . . .

. . . .

. . . .

. . . .

. . . .

. . . .

. . . .

. . . .

. . . .

. . . .

. . . .

. . . .

. . . .

2. Effort

9. Effort Activity: The 1–10 Scale

On a scale of one to ten

1 2 3 4 5 6 7 8 9 10

Look back at the work you've done so far this term and think about the levels of effort you've put in to your studies. Use the scale above and the following guideline to choose your number:

» 1: Little or no effort.

» 5: Some effort – you're working quite hard.

» 10: High levels of effort – the hardest you've worked.

Be honest with yourself, choose your number and record it in the box.

What Are Other Students Doing?

The problem with making a judgement about your own levels of effort is that scales can be subjective. Here are some of the issues:

» The numbers mean different things to different people.

» Students tend to surround themselves with people who do either similar or less work than they do. This means they 'normalise' the amount of work they are doing, even feel good about it, because they can point to someone doing less than they are.

» Students don't have a clear idea of what the hardest working students are doing.

» No one can know what students are doing in other colleges.

The answer is to get some concrete figures so the choice of number is a more accurate reflection of your levels of effort relative to other students.

Take another look at the 1–10 scale.

On a scale of one to ten

1 2 3 4 5 6 7 8 9 10

Look back at the work you've done so far this term and think about the amount of effort that you've put into your studies. Use the scale above and the following guideline to choose your number:

» 1: 0–2 hours' independent study a week.

» 5: 10 hours' independent study a week.

» 10: 20 hours' independent study a week.

Be honest with yourself, choose your number again and record it in the box.

We got these hourly figures by interviewing students. We've done it at a variety of levels; students taking their GCSEs report certain levels of effort, those taking A levels report other levels of effort. Your tutors and teachers will give you a sense of what high effort looks like in your context, so you might need to adjust these figures. Use them for now – they represent roughly what post-16 students do with their time.

What Can You Do?

First, reach 5/10. That means putting a timetable in place that takes you to ten hours of independent study per week. Use the space below to record your plans for stepping up your levels of effort. Shade out the times you're in college or otherwise engaged. Then examine how you might use the remaining time:

	9–10	10–11	11–12	12–1	1–2	2–3	3–4		6–7	7–8
M										
Tu										
W										
Th										
F										
Sa										
Su										

Go with this plan for a period of time! Studies say it takes thirty days to establish a habit. Start by aiming to make ten hours a week your habit for a month.

Then, in consultation with your tutors, step it up gradually. Go for twelve hours next, then fourteen. If you're doing twenty hours a week by the spring of your last year in college, we'd suggest you're in a really good place.

Final Thoughts

Remember – our studies show these are the hours the most successful students are doing. Don't fall for the myth of the brilliant, talented student who does superbly in every test without putting any effort in. We've never known it to be true – and we've worked with thousands of students. The ones with the best grades always turn out to be doing the most independent work!

10. Effort Activity: Working Weeks

In *The Recipe for Success* (2009), journalist and author Blaire Palmer interviewed hundreds of high earners and pulled together the qualities she found. There are, she reckons, ten key characteristics to success. She calls the tenth 'graft', by which she means just putting in the hours.

How Long Are the Working Weeks of High Earners in the UK?

As a student who takes all study periods as frees, you're on about twenty-three hours a week.

As a student who works all your frees, you're doing thirty-five hours a week.

A 9 to 5 working week amounts to forty hours a week.

The average UK worker does forty-three hours a week:

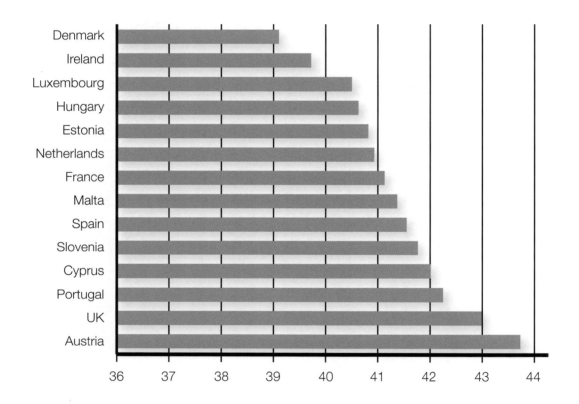

How do the hours on the chart above reflect your family's working patterns? Think about the working days your mum, dad, aunties or uncles have. What are their start and finish times? What are their holiday patterns?

. . . .

. . . .

. . . .

. . . .

More working week facts:

» The government recommends a maximum working week of forty-eight hours.

» High earners (top tax bracket of over £50K a year) average fifty hours a week.

» Company bosses interviewed worked between sixty and eighty hours a week.

What Does a Working Week Like That Look Like?

A fifty hour working week is …

Start each day at:	Take a lunch break from/to:	Go home at:

An eighty hour working week is …

Start each day at:	Take a lunch break from/to:	Go home at:

Final Thoughts

How many hours are you putting in on an average week? What is your holiday pattern like compared to a full time job? How do your hours compare to those of your parents, or to the average UK worker? How do you compare to yourself in Year 7 or 11?

Plan where you could get some extra hours from and use this grid to adjust your levels of effort upwards.

	9–10	10–11	11–12	12–1	1–2	2–3	3–4		6–7	7–8
M										
Tu										
W										
Th										
F										
Sa										
Su										

11. Effort Activity: The Three R's of Habit

Stanford University has a Persuasive Technology Lab. Here, academics study how interactive technology is changing our habits. Its founder and director, Dr B. J. Fogg, is studying how mobile phone technology can develop habit formation. Effort is also a habit. The level of effort you put into your study is a result of your habits. Some people have got the effort habit, some people haven't.

The argument goes that there are three elements to habit formation, often referred to as the three R's:

» **The reminder.** This could be a feeling, a place or a time of day – it's your body or brain giving you a trigger that initiates the behaviour. It might be getting some chocolate, going home early or putting away the work you know you should be completing.

» **The routine.** This is the behaviour itself. Going to the canteen and buying the chocolate or taking the bus home instead of staying on to do some studying. Often people will feel a twinge of guilt during the routine but do it anyway.

» **The reward.** This is the good feeling you get – the benefit you gain from engaging in the behaviour. It might not last long but it is a tempting prospect.

If you haven't currently got into the effort habit, how can you go about changing? You can use the three R's in your favour. Rather than thinking about stopping old habits – which is a mistake many people make when 'giving up' something – the trick is to think of it as starting a new habit. This means you will need a new reminder to trigger your new habit, a new routine to go through and, best of all, a new reward to give yourself!

Using the Habit-Planning Grid

» Choose a trigger attached to something that happens to you every day. For example, 'At the end of every lunch hour I will …', 'As I finish my breakfast I will …', 'As the bell for the end of the college day goes, I will …' or 'At the end of the 6 o'clock news I will …'.

» Choose a routine that is easy to achieve. It might be to sort out your notes for thirty minutes, review the assignment you've been set for thirty minutes or do one hour's work on a difficult subject. The key thing is this: in the beginning, performance doesn't matter. Routine matters.

» Finally, the reward. Start small with a verbal reward. It might be a 'Good work!' spoken aloud to yourself, a short period of time doing something you enjoy or a cup of coffee.

Reminder:	. . . .
	. . . .
	. . . .
Routine:	. . . .
	. . . .
	. . . .
Reward:	. . . .
	. . . .
	. . . .

Final Thoughts

It is far easier to establish a new habit than it is to break an old one. When you plan a new habit, never use the negative language associated with breaking habits. Avoid 'I must stop being lazy …' or 'I've got to give up skipping assignments …'. Instead, use positive language. Try, 'From Monday, I'm going to start working harder.'

Allow yourself slips and mistakes. They happen to everyone. Successful students keep going even when they've broken a habit. (Others make a mistake, then give everything up. Don't let this be you!)

Effort

12. Effort Activity: Recognising Your Blockers

A 'blocker' is a psychological barrier that stops you working. It might be a pattern of thinking or a habit you've established that you can't break. All of us have blockers – thoughts and feelings that stop us doing the thing we know we really need to do.

To put in the effort for success you have to recognise your blockers and break down those patterns of thought. This four stage model is useful for recognising the behaviours and thought patterns that are a sign of blockers.

1. Initial Lack of Motivation

Everyone feels discouraged at some point – the feeling that they don't want to complete a piece of work, finish an essay or put in a couple of hours on a tricky piece of coursework. The difference is what you tend to do next …

2. Bypassing Conscience

Most people will feel guilty when they don't work ('I should be finishing that essay …'), but sometimes we find ways of bypassing our conscience. We deliberately rethink the situation until we feel better about it. Some thought patterns you might have include:

» Student A hasn't done it either, so I'm not that bad.

» At other colleges they don't even do this piece, so why should I?

» The instructions were unclear, so I've got an excuse. I'm telling myself I didn't really understand.

» I rushed a piece last time and the grade was OK. I'll do that again.

» I deserve a break. I've always really loved this TV programme – I'll watch it instead.

» I'm going to do something else that has some 'educational value'.

3. Creating An Opportunity

Next, there needs to be something nearby that can distract you. Some students work near others and tell themselves this is beneficial because they can ask for help if they need it. What they might actually be doing is hoping for a distraction to occur. The same goes for workspaces. Do you work near or next to your phone, laptop, tablet, games console or TV, secretly hoping for something to take you away from your work? If this is you, then you are subconsciously (or maybe deliberately!) creating the opportunity for blocks to occur.

4. Getting Away With It

Finally, for the pattern to continue, you need to feel that you have got away with it. The thought pattern here often goes, 'Nobody said anything, so it must be alright' or 'I didn't get told off, so I'll do it again.'

This activity might help you recognise your own tendency to self-sabotage. Don't worry, everyone does it to a certain extent – really productive people have learned to fight the feeling!

Once you've noticed the ways in which your blockers get in the way, try the following:

» Think about a piece of work you never completed. How did you justify the non-completion to yourself? Which task on your list at the moment are you least likely to do? Why?

. . . .

. . . .

. . . .

. . . .

» Take a task that has been on your to-do list for a while because you've been putting it off. Why is it there? Is there an action you can take right away which will make the task suddenly achievable?

. . . .

. . . .

. . . .

. . . .

» Next time you put a task off, ask yourself why. Are you simply sequencing tasks and saving it for later? Or is this an act of self-sabotage?

Now that you've recognised some of your own blockers, make a plan for overcoming them. Record your observations and ideas here:

. . . .

. . . .

. . . .

. . . .

. . . .

Final Thoughts

Everyone has blockers – and everyone occasionally sabotages their own progress. The key is to recognise you're doing it, and to fight it! If you feel self-sabotage coming on, move location. Get yourself to a quiet room, a study area or the library. Start the task. You don't even have to finish it – work for thirty minutes or so – but get it started. You're less likely to sabotage a project that is already underway!

Effort

13. Effort Activity: Frogs and Banisters

This activity focuses on the separate advice of two academics. The 'frogs' part of this advice comes from time management guru Brian Tracy, who in *Eat That Frog!* (2013) asks his readers to imagine that tasks are frogs you have to eat. He chooses this metaphor because the thought of such tasks is often very off-putting. His advice is as follows: 'If you have to eat two frogs, eat the ugliest one first' (p. 2).

This is another way of saying that if you have important tasks to apply your effort to, start with the biggest, hardest and most important one first. This is related to Tim Ferriss' idea of the 'lead domino' (which he talks about in his podcast 'How to Build a Large Audience From Scratch (And More)' at http://fourhourworkweek.com): if you do the tough tasks first, your effort will be worthwhile because it will pay dividends later. So, list all your frog tasks – in order of ugliness!

The 'banisters' part comes from computer science professor Randy Pausch. 'It doesn't matter how well you polish the underside of the banister,' says Pausch (2010, p. 108). In other words, don't worry about unimportant details – put your effort where the result will be greatest.

List the work you've done recently. Have you been eating ugly frogs (getting tough, important jobs done) or have you been polishing the underside of the banister (half-heartedly completing easier looking jobs that aren't really important)?

Frogs	Banisters
. . . .	. . . .
. . . .	. . . .
. . . .	. . . .
. . . .	. . . .
. . . .	. . . .
. . . .	. . . .
. . . .	. . . .
. . . .	. . . .
. . . .	. . . .

Final Thoughts

Which jobs are you doing that you can stop?

. . . .

. . . .

. . . .

. . . .

. . . .

Which jobs are you avoiding that you should tackle?

. . . .

. . . .

. . . .

. . . .

. . . .

The thought of the work is often much worse than the work itself.

14. Effort Activity: The Ten Minute Rule

If you are in a position where you are regularly putting up barriers to work, the Ten Minute Rule is a good way of breaking them down. What do we mean by 'barriers'? Many students will avoid coursework or assignments because they are difficult. Instead they will:

» Do something more comfortable but less useful. They might copy out some notes or make a mind-map when really they know they should be doing the exam paper their tutor has set them under timed conditions.

» Claim that assignments or independent work 'aren't realistic' as a way of avoiding them. ('This is pointless. The real exam will be totally different so why bother?')

» Get into a deep discussion about something related so they feel like they are working.

» Look for someone else who isn't doing it. Or in extreme cases, tell themselves that no one is doing it.

You may recognise these behaviours in yourself and others – putting up barriers to independent work to avoid it.

If this is you, the Ten Minute Rule is a good way to break through barriers. It's very simple:

1 Tell yourself you are going to do ten minutes of intense work. That's all.

2 Decide what work the ten minutes is going to be spent on.

3 Clear a space and sit down with the right materials to hand.

4 Start.

You can, of course, stop after ten minutes. Even if you do, you've done ten minutes more work than you would have done. But what often happens is that ten minutes becomes twenty. Sometimes even half an hour or longer.

Final Thoughts

What do we learn from this experiment? Hopefully, you will realise that the thought of work is often much worse than the work itself. Try using the Ten Minute Rule with a task you are dreading.

Which task is currently the least pleasant on your to-to list? Plan to tackle it today. Use the Ten Minute Rule. Set yourself up somewhere quiet where you won't be disturbed, and go for it! Make your plans here:

. . . .

. . . .

. . . .

. . . .

. . . .

15. Effort Activity: Inner Storytelling

In *Better Than Before: Mastering the Habits of Our Everyday Lives* (2015), Gretchen Rubin, a lawyer and writer, says that the language we use to describe ourselves – our 'inner storytelling' – massively influences the amount of effort we put into a project.

Rubin argues that 'we tend to believe what we hear ourselves say, and the way we describe ourselves influences our view of identity' (2015, p. 225). Perhaps this describes you – maybe you've told yourself these stories for years. Inner storytelling helps us live up to our own hopes and fears.

Use this space to think about the stories you've told yourself. (Have you ever said, 'I'm not a good student' or 'I'm dim' or 'Other students are cleverer than me' or 'My problem is, I'm lazy'?)

. . . .

. . . .

. . . .

. . . .

. . . .

. . . .

For a week, your challenge is to change your inner storytelling. This, in turn, could well change your patterns of behaviour, your habits and, ultimately, the effort you put into your work. A good place to start would be to choose one of the following stories to tell about yourself:

» When I started college, I suddenly became a hard-worker. I battle.

» I give 100% whatever I do. I never give up.

» When I say I'll do something, I do it.

» I'll deliver. I always do.

» I don't waste time. I get things done.

» I'm dedicated and strong under pressure. People can rely on me.

» When there is a challenging task, I go at it until I'm done.

» I'm not lazy or flaky. I'm no shirker.

Once you've chosen your new story, you need to find a method of verbalising it. The word 'mantra' is often used to describe an utterance or phrase with psychological power. This is what you're creating here. Find a time of day when you can repeat your mantra – on the bus, in the shower, walking home or crossing the campus between lessons. Then try it for a week.

Record your mantra here:

. . . .

. . . .

When can you repeat this mantra to yourself? Think about bus journeys, waiting periods, silent study:

. . . .

. . . .

Final Thoughts

Simple, memorable mantras are best. Try creating a phrase – or even a list of words – that captures the kind of person you want to be.

16. Effort Activity: The Power of If … Then Thinking

Professor Peter Gollwitzer of New York University says that many people who want to put their efforts into achieving great things, but don't, are derailed by seemingly small problems like these:

» They want to finish a task to a high standard, but a phone call disrupts them.

» They want to complete a coursework piece, but the weekend is just too busy.

» They want to do some serious revision, but some friends disturb them and the work is abandoned.

In their book *The Psychology of Action* (1996), Peter Gollwitzer and John Bargh argue that if this happens to you, it's because you have low 'implementation intention' – you *sort of* want to put in the effort, but you will be easily put off if one thing goes wrong.

The solution? Successful students anticipate these problems and plan for how they will respond to them with maximum effort. You sequence actions that anticipate obstacles and build in pre-prepared solutions – you effectively beat self-sabotage before it even happens.

Consider these examples:

Student 1: 'I'll get started on this first thing in the morning.' This is a really common internal dialogue you might experience as a student – lots do it! And with one small disruption the whole plan comes to a standstill.

Student 2: 'I'll get started on this first thing in the morning. And …

» *If* I wake up late by accident, *then* I'll use my morning break to start it instead and …'

» *If* I feel really demotivated, *then* I'll get two coffees from the canteen and drink them quickly to give me a boost and …'

» *If* I get disturbed by friends, *then* I'll make an excuse and go to the library and …'

» *If* the internet is down, *then* I'll start by using my notes and save the research work until later.'

It's easy to see which student might be the one most likely to succeed. Student 2 has listed a series of potential problems and has recognised their tendency to self-sabotage when small things go wrong. By planning a change in action when those small obstacles come along, they are much more likely to keep pushing forward.

List all the usual blockers you use to prevent high levels of effort and for each one commit to a solution. Think them all through in your head and make notes. What you are doing is strengthening your implementation intention. You *will* put the effort in, even if small things crop up to stop you.

Use the table opposite to plan your response to self-sabotage:

If …	Then …
. . . .	. . . .
If …	Then …
. . . .	. . . .
If …	Then …
. . . .	. . . .
If …	Then …
. . . .	. . . .
If …	Then …
. . . .	. . . .

Final Thoughts

If … then planning often starts quite deliberately, with students using a grid like the one above to record their intentions. This keeps them firmly in mind when obstacles come.

But after a little while, you'll become good at internalising this kind of planning. You won't have to write it all down – you'll start doing it more instinctively. That's a great place to be.

An Effort Journal

The eight activities in this section have all been about establishing a link between success and hard work; about creating positive habits around the effort you put into your work; and about planning solutions to the problems of self-sabotage. Use this space to record your learning!

· ·

· ·

· ·

· ·

· ·

· ·

· ·

· ·

· ·

· ·

· ·

· ·

· ·

· ·

· ·

· ·

· ·

· ·

· ·

· ·

· ·

· ·

· ·

3. Systems

17. Systems Activity: The Energy Line

Many students feel overwhelmed by the amount of work they have to do. Some keep lists – scribbling down jobs and crossing them off when they're done. And lists are good – they help you keep on top of what it is you've got to do.

The drawback of a list is that it doesn't tell you what to do first. A better tool to use for prioritising tasks is an Energy Line – it beats a to-do list any day of the week. Scott Belsky suggests this technique in his book *Making Ideas Happen* (2011). We love it! It helps you put things in order according to how much effort you need to give them.

» **Step 1** – You start by listing all the tasks that you've got to do in the space below. Just empty your head of every task you can think of. Don't move onto step 2 until you are confident you've included everything.

» **Step 2** – This is where you prioritise the tasks. Put things on the left-hand side – high or extreme – if you need to work like mad on them. Put them on the right if you can kick back and leave it for a bit. Attach dates for submission and you're really getting there. You'll notice that there are a maximum number of tasks that you can include at the bottom of each column. For example, you can only have two tasks in the extreme column. It might be useful to use small sticky notes for each task, so that you can pull them off when you've completed.

Step 1 – List All the Tasks in the Box Below

Step 2 – Prioritise Your Tasks on the Table

Extreme	High	Medium	Low	Idle
Max: 2 tasks	Max: 4 tasks	Max: 8 tasks	Max: 4 tasks	Max: 2 tasks
. . . .	. . . .	. . . .	. . . .	. . . .
. . . .	. . . .	. . . .	. . . .	. . . .
	. . . .	. . . .	. . . .	
	. . . .	. . . .	. . . .	
		. . . .		
		. . . .		
		. . . .		
		. . . .		

Final Thoughts

Project management is the activity of planning and organising yourself and the resources you have in order to achieve long-term goals. The basic principles of project management aren't difficult and can be easily taught. You might not have thought about it like this, but your course is like planning four (or maybe more) projects.

How has this helped you think about how you prioritise your tasks?

. . . .

. . . .

. . . .

18. Systems Activity: The Breakfast Club

In *Sex Sleep Eat Drink Dream: A Day in the Life of Your Body*, Jennifer Ackerman (2008) shares some research which suggests that for most people, the brain is at its sharpest in the first four hours after waking. Not straightaway – it needs time to get up to speed. But then it hits a sweet spot when it's really firing. Brain efficiency can vary, she says, but in the morning it can be up to 30% more active and sharp than it is at other times.

Here's something else to consider: the longer the day goes on, the more self-control problems you will have. If you're trying to give up chocolate, for example, you will rarely crack at 10 a.m. But by 4.30 p.m., when you're feeling tired, your self-control slips. It's the same with work. If you tell yourself you will start a big project at 3 p.m. or 6 p.m., the chances of that happening are low. If you set aside some 'breakfast club' time – sweet spot time in the morning – you're much more likely to clear the job.

And yet we often see students using a morning study period to ease themselves into the day. They waste their moments of high brain energy on social media and gaming, then turn their attention to work later on when they're not as productive.

The Morning Routine

With all this in mind, look at your morning routine. Make some notes under the following headings:

» What time do you wake up?

....

» What do you do with your first hour?

....

....

....

....

» What are your habits and rituals, your repeated behaviours?

....

....

....

....

» Are they positive? Do they set you up for a good day?

....

....

....

....

» How long do they take? Are they worth it?

....

....

....

....

Scheduling

Now look at the work you have to do this week. Use the Energy Line to figure out what's coming up in terms of deadlines, then:

» Take your highest priority tasks (or your hardest or trickiest tasks) and schedule them in morning slots for the whole week.

» Commit to clearing them early in the day. Record your plans below:

Monday	Tuesday	Wednesday	Thursday	Friday
. . . .	. . . .	. . . .	. . . .	. . . .
. . . .	. . . .	. . . .	. . . .	. . . .
. . . .	. . . .	. . . .	. . . .	. . . .
. . . .	. . . .	. . . .	. . . .	. . . .
. . . .	. . . .	. . . .	. . . .	. . . .

Final Thoughts

What went well and what needs adjusting as a result of attending the 'breakfast club'?

....

....

....

....

....

19. Systems Activity: Snack, Don't Binge (or the Weekly Review)

Studies show that cramming or bingeing on learning isn't as successful as snacking on it. In other words, students do significantly better if they review their learning regularly rather than if they leave it to pile up, and then try to deal with it all at once. Your productivity – the amount of efficient and effective work you do – is significantly improved by doing the work frequently.

Here's a habit to work on developing. It's called the Weekly Review. Follow these steps and you will find yourself snacking – checking your learning regularly – instead of bingeing!

1 Set aside an hour a week. This time must be sacred – don't let anyone disturb you! Put your phone on aeroplane mode, go offline and never swap your hour for something else or skip it. Make it a crucial part of your week. We suggest a Friday afternoon or a Monday morning.

2 Split up the hour evenly. We suggest fifteen minutes per course. Be strict with yourself.

3 For fifteen minutes, review the week's work in that course. We suggest the following:

» Check your notes are clear, legible and in order.

» Summarise your learning in a quick diagram, mind-map or a few lines of notes.

» Highlight or circle material you've found hard this week. This is the stuff you will need to work on during your independent study time.

» Go through the jobs you've been given and the deadlines you've got. Make a prioritised list for the week ahead.

4 Once you've done this four times, once for each subject, you should be feeling pretty good. You're in control. You know what needs to be done.

Weekly Review – Reflections and Actions:

. . . .

. . . .

. . . .

. . . .

. . . .

. . . .

. . . .

. . . .

. . . .

. . . .

Final Thoughts

Students who make a habit of the Weekly Review are often much calmer and less stressed. They can leave college on Friday knowing they're on top of things. They've emptied their heads of all the little niggling worries that might keep them awake at night.

Which subject needs to be the one you do most regular reviews of? Why?

. . . .

. . . .

. . . .

20. Systems Activity: The 2–4–8 Rule

This is a simple system of time management. It's based on the idea of a long-term project being like a bridge. Imagine a bridge built over a wide valley. What kind of bridge are you imagining? We would bet it has vertical piers holding it up. That's because everyone knows that something which spans a long distance needs regular structure to support it.

Now imagine that bridge as a long-term project – an essay that needs to be handed in to your tutor in two weeks or a coursework project that needs to be submitted in three months. The project is a long-term, long-distance project, so it needs a regular structure to support it. The 2–4–8 rule helps you build that solid structure, like vertical piers supporting a bridge.

1. The Short-Term Project: 'You've got two weeks to complete this'

Many tutors might give you two weeks to complete a project. Here's how to use the 2–4–8 rule to respond:

» **Target 1: two days.** Make a note of what you would like to achieve to get the project started – a side of writing, three hours of reading, some research, organising your notes or planning your piece. Set yourself a target of two days to complete this work.

» **Target 2: four days later.** Make a note of where you want to be four days after that. Halfway through would be a sensible plan. Break the back of the task – get through the hard bit.

» **Target 3: eight days later.** You're handing in the assignment today. It needs to be complete. Make sure you've finished early, gone through it and made any adjustments.

2. The Long-Term Project: 'This needs finishing by March'

Often coursework submissions come with more extended deadlines like this. If your deadline is a longer one, it's worth working backwards from targets like this:

» **Target 3: eight months until submission.** In these early stages, you should be finding an example of what you're trying to achieve – for example, another student's coursework submission. Look it over and say to yourself, 'I want mine to look like this.' Make a list of what needs to be done by the end of the project. Get started on rough, early versions or drafts.

» **Target 2: four months until submission.** Make notes of where you would like to be halfway through assuming it's going really well. By now you will have been working on early versions and fleshing them out. How many sections will be complete in rough form by this point? What will your word count be (if it's a written task)? What reading and research will you have done and incorporated by this point? What standard will you have achieved?

» **Target 1: two months until submission.** If you've met your targets up to this point, you'll know very clearly what needs to be done to complete the project, and you can begin the final stages of the project in earnest. What groundwork do you still need to do? What reading needs to be completed? What notes do you still need to take and incorporate? How many words are left? How do you conclude and reference?

Delivery stage one:

Date: . . . .

To be complete: . . . .

. . . .

Notes: . . . .

. . . .

. . . .

Delivery stage two:

Date: . . . .

To be complete: . . . .

. . . .

Notes: . . . .

. . . .

. . . .

Delivery stage three:

Date: . . . .

To be complete: . . . .

. . . .

Notes: . . . .

. . . .

. . . .

Final Thoughts

Chunking large projects into smaller, more manageable tasks makes you feel less daunted about starting the project.

What projects are you currently working on that you could apply this strategy to? Make a list of these below:

. . . .

. . . .

. . . .

. . . .

. . . .

. . . .

21. Systems Activity: STQR

Successful project managers suggest you begin any huge project (like passing your college course) with an understanding of the following four things:

Scope	**Time**
The complete size of the finished project. What exactly do you need to learn?	How long have you got to do it by? Can you break this down into mini-deadlines?
. . . .	. . . .
. . . .	. . . .
. . . .	. . . .
. . . .	. . . .
. . . .	. . . .
. . . .	. . . .
. . . .	. . . .
. . . .	. . . .
Quality	**Resource**
What grade do you want? Have you any examples of work completed at this grade? Do you know students who have achieved it?	Who can help you? Tutors? Textbooks? Websites? The college VLE?
. . . .	. . . .
. . . .	. . . .
. . . .	. . . .
. . . .	. . . .
. . . .	. . . .
. . . .	. . . .
. . . .	. . . .
. . . .	. . . .

The first is scope – the size of the project. This is crucial: how big is the job ahead of you? Surprisingly, lots of students never really get to grips with what they need to know.

Second is the time frame. You need to consider two things here: when is the deadline for the project, and how many hours will you need to complete it? Thinking in terms of hours will give you a much clearer idea when it comes to scheduling the project.

Third is quality. Not only do you have to consider the standards you want to achieve, but you also need to know the criteria you are working towards. What exactly do you have to do to meet the standards? Write these down in this box.

Finally, in the resources box list everything you will need to complete the project. This can also include people – for example, you might have to meet certain tutors.

Final Thoughts

Once you've completed the STQR, take a photo on your phone, so that you can review your progress. You might also find it useful to do a 2–4–8 activity in the time box.

What one action could you complete today to get your project started?

. . . .

. . . .

. . . .

. . . .

. . . .

22. Systems Activity: Project Progress Chart

This is a simple tool to keep track of where you are with everything on which you're working. Whether you're taking three or four college courses, applying to university, organising some work shadowing or completing a re-take, the number of projects you're running at the same time can feel overwhelming. Don't worry. This is normal.

The Project Progress Chart helps you track where you are with each one. List every job or task you've got to do and place them somewhere on the grid. It will help you prioritise what to do next.

On the horizontal axis is *time*. Projects ahead of schedule go far right and projects lagging behind go far left. On the vertical axis is *quality*. Projects heading for a high quality finish go at the top and projects that are running on a low quality go towards the bottom.

QUALITY

High quality

·   ·

·   ·

·   ·

·   ·

·   ·

TIME

Behind schedule   Ahead of schedule

·   ·

·   ·

·   ·

·   ·

·   ·

Low quality

Final Thoughts

Take any task in the behind schedule/low quality quadrant – that's the bottom left one – and attach the length of time it would need to get them complete. Now go to your diary/planner and block out a period of time where you can make significant progress on these tasks.

The number of projects you're running at the same time can feel overwhelming. Don't worry. This is normal.

23. Systems Activity: The Eisenhower Matrix

This model was supposedly developed by US President Dwight Eisenhower – he was considered a master of time management, always getting everything done by the deadline. His famous alleged quote, 'I have two kinds of problems, the urgent and the important. The urgent are not important, and the important are never urgent,' led to the development of what is now referred to as the Eisenhower Matrix, which is used all over the world in business.

You start by making a list of all the tasks that you have to complete.

. . . .

. . . .

. . . .

. . . .

. . . .

. . . .

. . . .

. . . .

. . . .

. . . .

. . . .

. . . .

. . . .

. . . .

. . . .

. . . .

. . . .

Now try to organise your tasks using this framework.

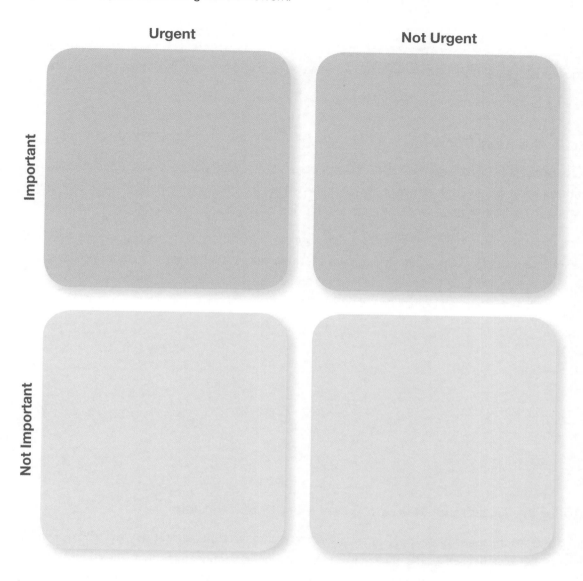

Urgent   **Not Urgent**

Important

Not Important

Eisenhower put all his tasks into one of four boxes on the matrix. He then dealt with the ones that were urgent and important. Only when all the tasks in this box were complete did he move on to the other boxes.

Final Thoughts

We like to consider urgency as how much time you have before a piece of work needs completing. So urgent tasks should have immediate deadlines. We define 'important' as tasks that will have a significant impact on your learning. If you know a task will definitely make you a more knowledgeable, more confident learner, categorise it as important.

Are there any tasks in the not urgent/not important box – the bottom right – that you could bin? Sometimes we have tasks on our to-do list that might not even need to be there!

24. Systems Activity: The Lead Domino

What Should I Focus My Time On?

Tim Ferriss, an entrepreneur and business adviser who is behind www.fourhourworkweek.com, recommends two tactics for helping you to decide where to focus your time to get maximum gains. He argues that a lot of work can be saved by focusing on jobs that will have the biggest knock-on effects.

These are the two principles he recommends when choosing your next task.

Go for the 'Lead Domino'

In his podcast, 'How to Build a Large Audience from Scratch (and More)', Ferriss argues that you should put your effort into the one job which, when done, will render the largest number of other jobs either easier or irrelevant. In other words, the job that has the largest number of positive knock-on effects.

When you've got a list of things to do, use this principle to guide where you put your effort. It will stop you (as Professor Randy Pausch puts it) 'polishing the underside of the banister' – in other words, spending time doing jobs that aren't necessary (see Frogs and Banisters on page 38 for extra advice on this one). Make a note of your Lead Dominoes – those big tasks that will have positive knock-on effects – below.

. . . .

. . . .

. . . .

. . . .

. . . .

Go for the Task Which Makes You Feel Most Uncomfortable

With this second piece of advice, Ferriss makes the point that, subconsciously, we often know which are the big, important jobs because they make us feel challenged or uncomfortable. There is a significant crossover between tasks that make us feel uncomfortable and tasks that are going to be important and improve us quickly.

The job that makes you feel anxious is likely to be your Lead Domino. And by focusing on it now, you will save time and effort later.

What's your most uncomfortable task?

. . . .

. . . .

. . . .

. . . .

. . . .

Final Thoughts

Block out some time and do your most uncomfortable task. If you can't bear the thought of starting it, use the Ten Minute Rule (page 41) to get you going!

Now, how did it make you feel when you completed that uncomfortable task?

. . . .

. . . .

. . . .

. . . .

. . . .

Return to this and read it next time you're having trouble starting!

A Systems Journal

The eight activities in this section have all been about project management. We much prefer this phrase to 'study skills', because project management is about sequencing and organising your resources, and your time. Use this space to record your learning.

. . . .

. . . .

. . . .

. . . .

. . . .

. . . .

. . . .

. . . .

. . . .

. . . .

. . . .

. . . .

. . . .

. . . .

. . . .

. . . .

. . . .

. . . .

. . . .

. . . .

. . . .

. . . .

4. Practice

25. Practice Activity: The Revision Questionnaire

We've found there is a strong link between the kind of revision someone does and the outcomes they get. So, which student will do better in an exam?

» Student 1 does fifteen hours' revision – all of it reading through notes.

» Student 2 only does ten hours' revision – two hours making mind-maps, two hours creating flash cards of key terms, three hours writing timed essays, two hours working through past papers and looking for patterns in the questions asked, and half an hour doing the hardest question they could find, followed by half an hour talking it through with their tutor. Then they spend five hours shopping with their friends and watching TV.

The second student will perform better, despite revising for fewer hours! You too can make less mean more. Try this questionnaire:

Subjects: _____

1 How many hours of independent work do you do on your subjects outside of college? Please state the time spent on each subject.

. . . .

. . . .

. . . .

2 What sort of activities do you do? Use the table below, ticking in the column which best describes your revision and preparation:

		Always	Sometimes	Never
Reading through notes	C			
Using resources on the college's VLE	C			
Using course textbooks	C			
Mind-maps/diagrams	C			
Making/remaking notes	C			
Highlighting/colour coding	C			
Flash cards	C			
Using a revision wall to display your learning	C			
Writing exam answers under timed conditions	S			
Reading model answers	S			
Using past exam questions and planning answers	S			
Marking your own work to a mark scheme	F			

		Always	Sometimes	Never
Studying mark schemes or examiners' reports	F			
Working with other students in groups/pairs	F			
Comparing model answers against your own work	F			
Creating your own exam questions	F			
Handing in extra exam work for marking	F			
One-to-one discussions with tutors	F			

3 Additional activities not mentioned above:

4 Write a brief account of what you do if you can't understand something (e.g. try again, read textbooks, check the college's VLE, see tutors, see other students).

. . . .

. . . .

. . . .

. . . .

Now check over your answers. You will notice some activities in the table have a 'C' next to them – these are the *content* techniques. Some activities have an 'S' next to them – these are the *skills* techniques. Others have an 'F' next to them – these are the *feedback* techniques.

Notice in our example that student 1 only does content revision, while student 2 does all three stages and then takes some time off. In our experience, student 2 will pretty much always get a better grade than student 1. And they put in fewer hours.

Make sure you do some revision for each of C, S and F! Aim for three of each; nine methods in total. Make a note of your current scores here:

» C score: . . . .

» S score: . . . .

» F score: . . . .

Final Thoughts

We've found that students who get the best grades at college practise in a wider variety of ways. Our top performers had over ten ticks in the always column, and these were pretty evenly spread across C, S and F.

However, students who did not perform well had far fewer ticks in the always column – often only four or five. They were very restricted in the way they practised, often spending hours repeating the same limited range of activities.

Aim to increase the ticks in your always column to ten.

List three activities that you currently don't do, that you could add to your repertoire:

. . . .

. . . .

. . . .

26. Practice Activity: Know the Skills

It's almost impossible to practise the component skills of a subject if you don't know what those skills are. Once you do know, you can put them into a target diagram like the one below. Target diagrams like this are used by sports psychologists when working with athletes.

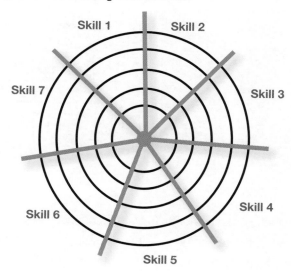

The slice of the target diagram is coloured in depending on how confident and practised you feel with a particular skill – a fully coloured in slice for a skill that you feel is fully developed and a totally empty slice for a skill that needs a lot of work.

Meet your tutors and ask them, 'What are the seven skills I need to master to get the top grade?' Read your syllabuses or course outlines and look at the assessment objectives (AOs), which are the skills the examiner is looking for. Then use the empty target diagrams in this section to begin a regular tracking of those skills:

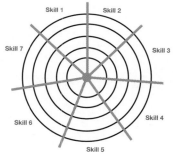

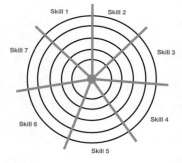

Subject: . . . .   Subject: . . . .   Subject: . . . .

Final Thoughts

Two ways we have seen students make very swift progress in a short space of time:

1 Ask your tutors for an example piece of work – it could be from another student – with the skills you want to improve demonstrated at whichever grade you want. Then analyse what is missing from your work.

2 Find a student you know who executes a particular skill better than you do, and work alongside them.

27. Practice Activity: Graphic Organisers

There is a difference between information and knowledge.

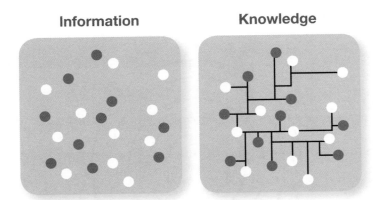

Information, on the left, is a loose collection of facts, with no connections between them, no overall understanding, so there is very little we can do with it. Information won't help you pass an exam or master a skill. On the right, you can see that knowledge is connected information. The job of any learner is to turn information into knowledge.

So how do we build these connections to turn information into knowledge? One way is by reorganising pieces of information.

Graphic organisers can help you do this. Some are very simple:

» Make a mind-map of the information.

» Make a comparison table and pull out similarities and differences between two studies, methods, people, characters or historical events.

» Make a flow chart to summarise a process or series of events.

» Make a graph to represent the data.

Notice the focus on action here – each of our suggestions begins with 'make'. That's you being active, engaging with information and reorganising it so it becomes knowledge.

Alternatively you can use complex graphic organisers. They usually take the form of a metaphor, where you turn something into something else.

For example, summarise everything you know about a topic using the metaphor of a tree:

» What key information forms the trunk?

» What underlying information makes the roots?

» What are the important branches?

» What subsections of information become the twigs and leaves?

If this metaphor works for you, try the following:

» A castle with separate turrets and a strong foundation.

» A stream growing into a river and then a lake.

» A village with a central square and streets around it.

Final Thoughts

By recasting and reorganising information, you're building strong neural connections in your brain, and really mastering the content of your subject.

But remember, mastering content is only the first step! The minute you feel confident, you must move on to skills practice and feedback. Check the Revision Questionnaire on page 66 to see what activities you should be completing next.

28. Practice Activity: The Leitner Box

The Leitner Box, which was developed by a German scientist called Sebastian Leitner, is a really effective, easy-to-develop practice and recall system. It's based on using flash cards to learn and then recall information, so this activity will need a whole bunch of subject-related flash cards. The cards are used as normal to record quick, easy-to-read bullet-pointed information about topics.

Leitner suggests that when we have a large amount of information to learn on flash cards, we have a tendency to gravitate towards the cards we already know and subconsciously avoid those we find difficult. To circumvent this, you create four subsections in your box (or four separate boxes):

» **Box 1.** Here you put items for frequent practice. This is the stuff you're not remembering well – it needs regular review and rereading because you're making mistakes when you practise recalling it or you don't know it at all. Around 40% of your time should be spent hammering the content of these cards. When you score a victory and fully recall a card, you move it down to box 2.

» **Box 2.** About 30% of your time is spent here. It's the stuff you've only just moved out of box 1 or learning that still trips you up or confuses you in any way. This material should be moving up (if you're not remembering it) or down (if you've nailed it) fairly regularly.

» **Box 3.** You spend 20% of your time here, and you nearly always get this stuff correct when you test yourself on it. You feel confident, even when the material is complex. However, if you dip in here and make any mistakes in recall at all, the card must be moved into box 2.

» **Box 4.** You begin with only a small number of cards here. This is the material you consider easy. You always get it right, so you only need to spend 10% of your time checking stuff in this box. However, and this is key, nothing ever leaves this box because you know it so well. No matter how confident you feel, you still check it every now and again.

If you practise your recall in this way, you will find you won't neglect information. You won't get caught by the 'familiarity trap' – the feeling that you know something so well you never need to test yourself on it. Plus, you keep your focus where it needs to be: on the tough stuff you keep forgetting. Use the grid below to plan what information might belong in each box:

Box 1: 40% of your time	Possible topics:
	. . . .
	. . . .
	. . . .
	. . . .
	. . . .

Box 2: 30% of your time	Possible topics:
	. . . .
Box 3: 20% of your time	Possible topics:
	. . . .
Box 4: 10% of your time	Possible topics:
	. . . .

Final Thoughts

If there's one quality we've seen that differentiates top performing students from others, it's the courage and determination to spend time focusing on weaknesses. This activity helps you isolate where your attention needs to be. It may be uncomfortable, but it will make a huge difference to your levels of performance!

29. Practice Activity: Two Slow, One Fast

This idea is borrowed from the sporting world. In sport, the word 'drill' is often used to describe practice. A drill is a specific and focused practice where all the chaos and uncertainty of the actual game is removed. Instead, a single skill is focused on and repeated. After some time working on a drill, players might then play a game in which the particular skill is tested.

Does this work with study too? With a maths problem or a history essay? The answer is yes.

» **Go slow.** To begin with you should try the equivalent of a drill. You're taking out the stress, worry and complexity, so you're not thinking about the chaos and uncertainty of doing an exam. You're going slowly, paying attention to what you do. That might mean taking half an hour to work through a short answer exam question, twenty minutes on a maths problem, an hour on a couple of science questions or half an hour writing a single killer paragraph for an essay.

» **Go fast.** Then you can try to apply the learning in a 'game' situation – in other words, under exam conditions. Pick an exam question, work out how long you would have in the exam and see whether you can perform at the same level but under the pressure of time.

Two Slow, One Fast describes the best sequence for developing a skill. Do it twice slowly and safely, paying attention to exactly what you're doing and why you're doing it. Then do it fast and see how you cope. You won't be perfect first time, but you will certainly accelerate the speed at which you get better.

Which subjects might this work best with?

Think about your studies at the moment, and make a list of the exam tasks you have ahead of you, that could be intensively practised using the two slow, one fast technique:

. . . .

. . . .

. . . .

. . . .

. . . .

Final Thoughts

Try combining this activity with Right, Wrong, Right, on the next page. Together, they make a powerful combination!

30. Practice Activity: Right, Wrong, Right

One way to burn understanding into your brain, particularly a skill, is to find someone who does it well. It might be your tutor or a fellow student, someone in your class or someone in the year above. Find an example of them doing it right. It might be a complex mathematical problem worked through, a definition and example question, a perfect paragraph of explanation or an analysis of a table of data.

Once you've got the example, you can do the following activity. We've found it works well at helping students see the difference between a successful answer and unsuccessful answer by making you focus on the differences between wrong and right.

The principle is very simple. It goes like this:

1 Using your example, copy the skill. You must do it right. It might be that you write a paragraph that borrows the best bits from the example you've got, or you might solve a very similar mathematical problem following your example.

2 Then do it wrong. Do it the way you've been doing it. Examine the differences. Where exactly do you go wrong? What is the result of that error? Where does it lead? How does wrong look different?

3 Then copy the skill right again.

You go – right, wrong, right. The two rights start to burn the understanding into your brain. The wrong in the middle helps you see why the wrong is wrong.

Isolating the Errors

It's worth spending some time looking at the differences between the two rights and the wrong. Try to make a list of three or four things that the right is doing that the wrong wasn't. Make a note of them here:

. . . .

. . . .

. . . .

Final Thoughts

A simple way to summarise your learning here is to record:

» Something you need to do more of. (More regular quotation? More academic terminology? More references to studies? More evaluation of sources? More careful checking of calculations?)

» And something you need to do less of. (The opposite of the suggestions above.)

More of:

. . . .

Less of:

. . . .

Practice

31. Practice Activity: Learning from Mistakes

Professor James Reason of the University of Manchester has done a lot of work about mistakes that lead to disasters (aeroplane crashes, mistakes in surgery, etc.). His findings can be applied to mistakes we make whenever we do something challenging. Luckily, the mistakes you make don't have any serious consequences – at least not compared to an air crash.

If you want to accelerate the speed at which you get good at something, it helps if you do the following:

1 Make mistakes. This may sound obvious but some students feel frightened or depressed when they make mistakes, so they avoid making them. If a piece of work is difficult and they are likely to make lots of mistakes, they copy someone else's or 'forget' to hand it in. You must make mistakes so you can learn from them.

2 Once the error is made, grab it. Mistakes are information. Don't ignore them, hide them or quickly correct them. Study them.

3 Categorise your mistake and work out why it happened. Professor Reason argues that there are three broad reasons for error:

Type of mistake	Possible response
1. Active mistake The wrong process is carried out (e.g. the calculation goes wrong because an incorrect approach is used, the mark scheme isn't present, the student doesn't know what to do to get a high mark).	Examine processes. Categorise them. Attach processes to problems – are you using the right one?
2. Slip-up The correct process is chosen but errors in the execution of that process lead to a lower mark (e.g. a paragraph lacks detail or is missing a key component, a science or maths solution works up to a point and then breaks down).	Practise the process. Collect examples of the process being done well.
3. Blackout The information needed to complete the challenge is either missing or forgotten.	Review notes and knowledge. Check another student's notes. Use course textbooks to strengthen learning. Strengthen recall through revision techniques.

Try categorising your errors, then draw up a list of actions you could take to reduce the chances of that error occurring again. Use the table below.

A level subject:

Type of mistake	Actions:
1. Active mistake The wrong process is carried out (e.g. the calculation goes wrong because an incorrect approach is used, the mark scheme isn't present, the student doesn't know what to do to get a high mark).	. . . .
2. Slip-up The correct process is chosen but errors in the execution of that process lead to a lower mark (e.g. a paragraph lacks detail or is missing a key component, a science or maths solution works up to a point and then breaks down).	. . . .
3. Blackout The information needed to complete the challenge is either missing or forgotten.	. . . .

Final Thoughts

Just the act of getting all your feedback together in one place is a fantastically useful activity. Many students have lots of tutor feedback, but it's scattered across nine or ten different pieces of work jammed into bags or stranded in different files.

Audit your feedback and you stand a much better chance of working effectively on your weaknesses.

Practice

32. Practice Activity: Mechanical vs. Flexible

A recent experiment undertaken with students at The Blue Coat School has a lot to tell us about practice.

All the students were set the same task – they had to throw a rolled-up ball of paper into a bin from three yards. They all knew they had to practise and that they would be tested on the number of successful throws they achieved at the end of the practice period. Here's the interesting bit: group 1 were told to repeat three yard throws over and over again, and group 2 were made to alternate between two yard and four yard throws over and over again.

When the two groups were brought back together to do a three yard bin throw, it's worth pointing out that group 1 had done hundreds of three yard bin throws. Group 2 hadn't practised any three yard bin throws at all.

Then we slightly adjusted the position of the bin – only by a few inches. Which was more successful? Group 2. Why? There is a difference between mechanical practice and flexible practice. Mechanical practice doesn't change – it repeats the same thing over and over. Flexible practice builds in different levels of challenge; the two yard throw is easier and the four yard throw is significantly harder.

What Does This Mean for A Level Study?

Those students who practise mechanically (group 1 students) can have nightmare exam experiences. They will often say, 'The question was slightly different! It totally messed with my concentration! I didn't know what to do!'

Students who practise flexibly (group 2 students) start to think flexibly. They will say, 'The questions were a bit weird. Eventually I worked out what I needed to do though.'

Make sure you mix it up in practice. Challenge yourself to:

» Seek out the weirdest questions that have ever come up and try them.

» Create strange questions.

» Visit the website of a different exam board and try their questions instead.

Record your observations here.

Subject: . . . .   Topic area: . . . .

Standard exam question	Harder variation of standard	Weirdest exam question ever!
. . . .	. . . .	. . . .
. . . .	. . . .	. . . .
. . . .	. . . .	. . . .
. . . .	. . . .	. . . .
. . . .	. . . .	. . . .

Now you can stay flexible in your practice!

Final Thoughts

These weird, unpredictable exam questions are sometimes referred to as 'curveballs'. They're disorientating and can derail even confident students. But challenging, flexible practice will mean you can cope.

We always fondly remember an ace mathematician we worked with. On the day of his final exam he was supremely confident – convinced there wasn't a curveball he hadn't already seen. And he was right; he didn't drop a single mark. Afterwards, when we interviewed him, it turned out the exam he'd just taken was the fifteenth paper he'd completed under timed conditions in the fortnight before the exam.

You too can be that well prepared!

A Practice Journal

The eight activities in this section have all been encouraging you to think about what good practice is. You should be ensuring you move away from content revision as soon as you can, and you should be focusing relentlessly on your weaknesses. Sometimes it's uncomfortable, but it's worth it! Use this space to record your learning.

5. Attitude

33. Attitude Activity: Force Field Analysis

Force Field Analysis is a method for listing, discussing and assessing the various forces for and against a proposed challenge you are facing. It helps you look at the big picture by analysing all of the forces impacting on you and weighing up the pros and cons. Having identified these, you can then develop strategies to reduce the impact of the opposing forces and strengthen the supporting forces. So, if you are finding it difficult to motivate yourself towards a certain aspect of your studies, this might be one for you.

Forces that help you achieve the challenge are called 'driving forces'. Forces that work against the challenge are called 'restraining forces'. Chart the forces by listing, in strength scale, the driving forces on the left and the restraining forces on the right. The important thing to do is to make sure the driving forces are more compelling than the restraining forces.

Have a go with a challenge you're facing.

The Challenge

Driving forces ⟶	Current state	⟵ Restraining forces
. . . .		. . . .
. . . .		. . . .
. . . .		. . . .
. . . .		. . . .
. . . .		. . . .
. . . .		. . . .
. . . .		. . . .
. . . .		. . . .
. . . .		. . . .
. . . .		
. . . .		
. . . .		
. . . .		
. . . .		

Final Thoughts

You'll notice we've given you fewer lines to record your restraining forces. This is because, psychologically, you need to have a longer list of positive, driving forces. This longer list will help you go into a challenge with a more positive attitude!

Is there one thing you can do that will remove a restraining force from your list? Take the action now.

. . . .

. . . .

. . . .

34. Attitude Activity: Stopping Negative Thoughts

In his 1998 book, *How to Stubbornly Refuse to Make Yourself Miserable About Anything*, American psychologist Albert Ellis looked at irrational and negative thinking experienced by people in times of stress. He particularly looked at types of thoughts that people experience when things go badly. He called this 'crooked thinking'.

His work can be directly applied to students in stressful situations – see if you've experienced these kinds of thoughts when things go wrong:

» Not fair thinking: 'I don't deserve this treatment. Things shouldn't be like this.'

» Catastrophe thinking: 'If this goes wrong, it'll be a total nightmare.'

» Stopper thinking: 'I'm useless. I can't do this. I'm bound to screw up.'

» Illogical thinking: 'If this bad thing happens, this one will surely follow.'

» Blaming thinking: 'It's his fault. It's everyone's fault except me.'

» Overgeneralising: 'I never get the breaks. This always happens to me. Everything is going wrong in my life.'

Are any of these thoughts familiar to you? Record and categorise the kind of negative thoughts you sometimes experience:

. . . .

. . . .

. . . .

. . . .

Ellis argued that the first step was for the individual to recognise when they were slipping into negative thinking. Once they could do that, his suggestion was 'reframing the thought positively'. He said this meant being hard on yourself. Only one person could be in charge of your thoughts – you. So you have to be firm, strong and not take any nonsense.

» Not fair thinking becomes: 'I did what I could. It's a setback but I can handle it.'

» Catastrophe thinking becomes: 'I'm going to perform well. I'm well prepared.'

» Stopper thinking becomes: 'I'm learning. I'm getting better each time I hit a challenge like this.'

» Illogical thinking becomes: 'There's no direct connection between this and that. The past does not equal the future. Tomorrow's another day.'

» Blaming thinking becomes: 'It's happened now. It doesn't matter whose fault it was. The important thing is to move on and learn from it.'

» Overgeneralising becomes: 'There are a few problems I'm dealing with at the moment. Everyone has tough times and I'm no exception. But I know I'm strong enough to cope.'

Now take one of the negative thoughts you recorded above, and try to reframe it, using the examples above:

. . . .

. . . .

. . . .

. . . .

. . . .

. . . .

These are the kinds of thoughts you might find yourself, or hear others, expressing in difficult times. Take the statements below and see how you might reframe them into something more positive:

» I've never been good at exams.

» Stuff like this always happens to me.

» If my report is bad, my mum and dad are going to hate me.

» I'm only going to fail, so what's the point in trying?

» The tutor doesn't like me.

» Nothing goes right for me. Why should geography be any different?

» I've been rubbish at science since primary school. I should have never picked it to study in college.

» I'm not going to get the result I need to reach my next goal, so I'll end up without a job and have a miserable life.

» If I fail this mock, it will mean the whole term has been a disaster.

» This is typical of my life. Nothing is easy or straightforward. I'm sick of it.

Final Thoughts

Like anything worthwhile, reframing thoughts takes practice. But you'll be surprised how quickly you can turn yourself into someone much more positive and optimistic.

Your friends and peers are an important contributing factor to your mood. Have a look at The Vampire Test on page 95 for more on this.

35. Attitude Activity: Kill Your Critic

Popular psychology regularly refers to the 'inner critic' – the voice we all have inside our heads that pokes fun at our achievements, hopes and dreams. Some people have inner critics with such strong voices that they are too scared to commit to anything – we've worked with students who couldn't bring themselves to admit (even to a tutor or parent) what their dream or goal was.

If this is you, try the following activities to improve your confidence in yourself. Killing your critic isn't easy, but there are some ways forward.

» Name your critic. Seriously. Some students find it easier to dismiss the voice if they've given it a silly name.

. . . .

» Listen to it – recognise its voice. Next time you hear it, label it: 'That's my inner critic.' At least you will start recognising it. What is it fond of saying?

. . . .

. . . .

. . . .

» Kill all comparisons. Let the inner critic say what it wants for ten minutes but all comparisons are banned. If it tries telling you, 'You're not as good as …' shut it down. It's called 'impostor syndrome' when you feel you are a fraud. 'I don't deserve to be here' or 'Others are cleverer than me' are common feelings and messages. Refuse to accept the voice if it tries any comparisons like these. Design a response – a quick, no-nonsense answer that shuts your critic down:

. . . .

. . . .

. . . .

. . . .

» Challenge your inner critic with data, such as your GCSEs or the last grade you got on a piece of work. Or challenge your inner critic with a demand: 'Well, if you think that, what should I do about it? Got any ideas?' Use the space below to record your successes:

. . . .

. . . .

. . . .

. . . .

» Start working on something new but tell your inner critic you're just messing about. This is apparently a tactic used regularly in advertising and movie writing. You say to yourself, 'I'm just messing around here, making a few sketches or writing a few words. It's just a bit of fun …' What have you been too afraid to start work on before now?

. . . .

. . . .

. . . .

» Invite it to come back at another time. This is a good one. You say, 'I'd appreciate your constructive criticism when this is finished.' Set a date and write it down. Say to yourself, 'I'll listen to my critic – in a week's time for fifteen minutes.'

. . . .

. . . .

. . . .

Final Thoughts

Everyone has an inner critic – you're not alone. As long as you can manage the negative thoughts, you'll do extremely well. Your tutors will have felt the same at some point, as will your peers, or parents, or family. How have they coped? It will be worth asking them for their tricks and tactics!

Use the space below to make some initial plans about beating your inner critic:

. . . .

. . . .

. . . .

. . . .

. . . .

. . . .

. . . .

. . . .

36. Attitude Activity: There and Back

This activity has been used successfully with adults experiencing difficulties in their work or personal life. It's a balancing exercise that frees up the mind and lets you make sense of hundreds of competing thoughts, ideas, worries and fears. So, if you're in a muddle, if you're struggling to feel positive or if you're feeling gloomy, this one might work for you.

The human brain works more effectively with good blood flow, so walking is essential to this activity. After your walk, you will need half an hour to collect your thoughts, jotting things down and making notes. Alternatively, you can use the voice recorder on a mobile phone to record your thoughts and ideas as you go. For this activity to work, you need to be disciplined and follow these rules to the letter!

Block out an hour of your time. You must be alone and undisturbed for this hour. Choose a destination that is about twenty minutes' walk away. While you walk there, you can only think positive thoughts. Your topic is: things I am good at and things I am thankful for. Nothing else can enter your mind. Bully yourself into staying on these two topics. Record your thoughts or list them quickly on a notepad.

Then turn around and return to your start point. While you walk back, you can address the problems you think you have, but here is the rule – your topic is: things I can do to solve my problems. Be strong with yourself. This is the only thing you can think about. When you arrive back, take a few minutes alone and make a note of your thoughts and ideas.

A final thought: worry is a call to action. If you're worrying, make a list of actions and then act on what you have listed. If you don't change things, things don't change.

Some people repeat this activity a couple of times a month to help them refocus. One person we know has the top of a hill as their destination – they say that walking down it helps them to relax after the hard slog of getting to the top, and they always come up with actions they can take to solve problems on the way down.

'Walking there' (things I am good at; things I am thankful for)	'Walking back' (things I can do to solve my problems)
. . . .	. . . .
. . . .	. . . .
. . . .	. . . .
. . . .	. . . .
. . . .	. . . .
. . . .	. . . .
. . . .	. . . .
. . . .	. . . .
. . . .	. . . .

Final Thoughts

This is a very satisfying activity if you finish it with an action – something you've listed in the right-hand column – that you do as soon as you get back.

Repeat the activity even if your lists remain the same. The recording of positives on the left, and plans on the right, is very inspiring!

37. Attitude Activity: Failing Forwards

American journalist Dan Coyle (author of *The Talent Code* and *The Little Book of Talent*) argues that mistakes are information. He says that those who have become brilliant at something have got better at it quickly because they have made a lot of mistakes and they have paid attention to their mistakes and drawn the learning out from them.

So, failure is important if we are ultimately going to succeed. There are, however, different attitudes to failure. Some students hate it and avoid it at all costs. It makes them feel embarrassed, humiliated, worthless. They hide mistakes or don't complete tests so they can avoid failing. As a result they make slower progress.

Other students recognise the importance of failure. Your job is to try to become one of these people. John Maxwell puts it this way in his book *Failing Forward* (2012): some people fail backwards (the failure takes them in a backwards direction), whereas some people fail forwards (the failure accelerates their progress).

Have a look at the characteristics Maxwell associates with these different types of failing in the table below.

Failing backwards	Failing forwards
Blaming others.	Taking responsibility.
Repeating the same mistake.	Learning from each mistake.
Expecting never to fail.	Knowing failure is part of the process.
Expecting to fail continually.	Maintaining a positive attitude.
Accepting tradition blindly.	Challenging outdated assumptions.
Being limited by past mistakes.	Taking new risks.
Thinking 'I am a failure'.	Believing something didn't work.
Withdrawing effort.	Persevering.

Now try to adapt your thinking so that it takes in the statements from the right-hand column.

» Take a recent failure and describe it in a paragraph. It might be a test, essay or assignment that went badly.

» Now look at your tutor's feedback. What are they picking out as areas of weakness? Make some notes about this, rephrasing their feedback in your own words.

» Finish by making a simple list: what are you going to do differently next time?

A recent failure:

. . . .

. . . .

. . . .

. . . .

. . . .

. . . .

The feedback I got:

. . . .

. . . .

. . . .

. . . .

. . . .

Next time I need to:

. . . .

. . . .

. . . .

. . . .

. . . .

Final Thoughts

Look at Maxwell's descriptions of 'failing backwards'. Which of these are most like you? If you could pick one that you feel you need to stop doing which would it be? What are you going to do instead?

. . . .

. . . .

. . . .

. . . .

Attitude

The Change Curve is based on a model originally developed in the 1960s by psychologist Elisabeth Kübler-Ross to explain the phases people go through during the grieving process. Kübler-Ross proposed that a terminally ill patient would progress through certain stages of grief when informed of their illness. Nowadays, the curve is used to help people understand their reactions to significant change in their lives.

Starting study in college is a significant change in any student's life and, like any change, it's likely that you will experience some of the following feelings.

The Change Curve

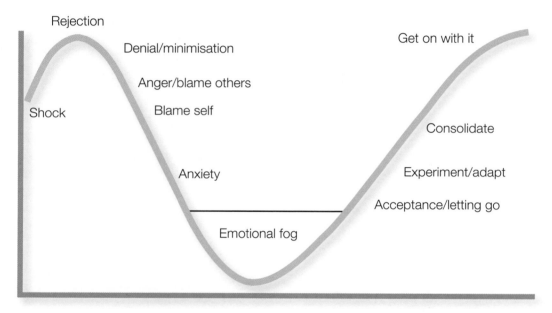

Think about your responses to college work. We've heard things like this:

» **Rejection:** 'I don't believe what you're telling me about college study. It doesn't seem any different. I'll carry on as normal.'

» **Denial/minimisation:** 'I'm fine. It'll be alright. Stop hassling me about how different it is.'

» **Anger:** 'I actually hate this. The tutors are rubbish. The subjects are nothing like they said they would be. I wish I'd never started, or gone to that other college.'

» **Blame self:** 'It turns out I'm just not clever enough to do this.'

» **Anxiety:** 'Everyone else is better than me. I'm missing deadlines. I'm not sleeping well. I don't understand the work. I'm not enjoying this challenge at all. I'm scared I'll fail.'

» **Emotional fog:** Withdrawing effort. Giving up.

» **Acceptance/letting go:** 'Things are different now. It's hard, but I'm getting to grips with it.'

» **Experiment/consolidate/get on with it:** 'I'm getting better at this. My grades aren't great but they're improving. There are some parts of these courses I like.'

Look at the examples above, and think about where you are on the curve. Then think about your friends too. Are they in different places?

. . . .

. . . .

. . . .

. . . .

. . . .

How does this help? First, you're not alone. Everyone goes through these feelings. Acknowledge and accept them. Second, some students go faster than others, but for most people it takes until the spring to get through the fog. Third, wherever you are on the curve, keep your eyes on the next stage. You *will* get there!

Final Thoughts

We've seen students get stuck in an early phase of the change curve for a long time – weeks and months – where they repeat the same complaints and worries.

If this is you, or someone you know, try Stopping Negative Thoughts on page 84.

You are the average of the five people you spend the most time with.

Jim Rohn

39. Attitude Activity: The Vampire Test

Jim Rohn is an entrepreneur and writer who studies success. In essence, he argues that those who surround themselves with good people become good – those who surround themselves with hard working people become hard working. Equally, those who surround themselves with lazy people become lazy.

This is something we see every year: promising students who have a friendship group which almost enforces disengagement. The group will effectively mock or punish any group member who is enjoying study, succeeding or working hard. It's sometimes difficult to tell if it's happening to you, and by the time you've figured it out it can be too late.

Taking the Test

Writer and artist Austin Kleon has a solution. He calls it the Vampire Test, and he explains it in his book, *Show Your Work!* Kleon advises that 'if, after hanging out with someone you feel worn out and depleted, that person is a vampire. If, after hanging out with someone you still feel full of energy, that person is not a vampire' (2014, p. 129).

Think about the five people you spend most time with and ask yourself five questions about them:

» Are they positive people?

» Do they enjoy their lives?

» Are they a good influence?

» Have they helped you through problems?

» Do they make you feel good about yourself and about life?

If you answer 'no' to these questions, can you list the names of people who might be better students to spend time with?

. . . .

. . . .

. . . .

. . . .

. . . .

. . . .

. . . .

. . . .

. . . .

Final Thoughts

We've seen students who are feeling negative about the challenges of study respond by surrounding themselves with negative people so they can wallow in complaining. You must guard against this, because it makes you feel as if 'everyone hates studying', and normalises your negativity. Think of a student who seems more positive, happy or energetic, and try to align yourself with them instead.

40. Attitude Activity: Stand Tall

If you're a football fan, what do you do when your team scores a goal? What do you do if you win when playing a game or when listening to your favourite band? For most people the answer is to stand up tall with their arms outstretched – something similar to the pose you often saw Usain Bolt adopt as he crossed the 100 metre finish line.

Amy Cuddy, a social psychologist at Harvard University, has looked at why people adopt this pose and the effects it can have on your physiology. She has found that by changing your physiology (or your posture) you can have a profound effect on how you feel. In her 2012 TED talk, 'Your Body Language Shapes Who You Are', she argues that by standing in certain 'power poses' you can increase your confidence and self-esteem, enhance your memory and reduce feelings of fear.

Cuddy goes on to argue that weaker postures (such as curling up, making yourself small or moving into defensive positions) trigger other psychological responses – feelings of imminent danger, stress or threat. And yet we often see nervous students hunched over their notes or hiding in a corner in those last few moments before an exam!

Instead, we think it's worth trying more confident and powerful postures before taking your final exams or important assessments.

Here's how you do it:

Power Pose 1

Stand tall with your hands on your hips and elbows pointing out. Your feet should be approximately one foot apart. Look straight ahead and think of a time you felt confident, strong and in control. Hold the pose for as long as you can. Aim for five minutes. You may need to begin with two or three minutes and build up.

Power Pose 2

You will need a little more space for this one. Stand as above, but this time put your arms above your head, stretched out like the arms of a clock at the 10 to 2 position. Again, hold your head high, stick your chest out and think about a time you felt really confident. And again, if you can, hold the pose for five minutes.

These poses are positive and confidence building – but not ones you might feel comfortable doing in public. Therefore, don't think of this as an activity you can only do outside an exam hall. We've found standing tall can also benefit students when they hit a block in their revision.

So, next time you're working away in your room and you hit a block, don't hunch yourself over your notes. Take a break and stand in the power pose!

Final Thoughts

Many professionals talk about the importance of energy, movement, exercise and positivity to break up a challenging working day.

Take some time to schedule in a walk, a run, a session at the gym or a power pose. Is there a particular time of the week you could do this?

An Attitude Journal

The eight activities in this section have all been about establishing a link between your thoughts, your attitude and your response to setbacks. The toughest, most positive students will be the ones who succeed. That can be you! Use this space to record your learning.

. . . .

. . . .

. . . .

. . . .

. . . .

. . . .

. . . .

. . . .

. . . .

. . . .

. . . .

. . . .

. . . .

. . . .

. . . .

. . . .

. . . .

. . . .

. . . .

. . . .

. . . .

. . . .

. . . .

. . . .

Further Reading

We'd recommend having a look through the following books for further inspiration. Check out your college library and ask for copies to be ordered in – they'll be happy to oblige.

Ackerman, J. (2008). *Sex Sleep Eat Drink Dream: A Day in the Life of Your Body* (New York: Mariner Books).

Allen, D. (2002). *Getting Things Done: How to Achieve Stress-Free Productivity* (London: Piatkus).

Belsky, S. (2011). *Making Ideas Happen: Overcoming the Obstacles Between Vision and Reality* (New York: Penguin).

Coyle, D. (2009). *The Talent Code: Greatness Isn't Born. It's Grown. Here's How* (New York: Bantam).

Coyle, D. (2012). *The Little Book of Talent* (London: Random House).

Duhigg, C. (2014). *The Power of Habit: Why We Do What We Do in Life and Business* (New York: Random House).

Dweck, C. (2007). *Mindset: The New Psychology of Success* (New York: Ballantine Books).

Ellis, A. (1998). *How to Stubbornly Refuse to Make Yourself Miserable About Anything (Yes, Anything!)* (New York: Citadel Press).

Foer, J. (2012). *Moonwalking with Einstein: The Art and Science of Remembering Everything* (London: Penguin).

Gollwitzer, P. M. and Bargh, J. A. (eds) (1996). *The Psychology of Action: Linking Cognition and Motivation to Behavior* (New York: Guilford Press).

Kleon, A. (2014). *Show Your Work! 10 Things Nobody Told You About Getting Discovered* (New York: Algonquin Books).

Lemov, D. (2012). *Practice Perfect: 42 Rules for Getting Better at Getting Better* (San Francisco, CA: Jossey-Bass).

Martin, A. (2010). *Building Classroom Success: Eliminating Academic Fear and Failure* (London: Continuum).

Maxwell, J. (2012). *Failing Forward: Turning Mistakes into Stepping Stones for Success* (Nashville, TN: Thomas Nelson Publishing).

Oettingen, G. (2014). *Rethinking Positive Thinking: Inside the New Science of Motivation* (New York: Penguin).

Palmer, B. (2009). *The Recipe for Success: What Really Successful People Do and How You Can Do it Too* (London: A&C Black).

Pausch, R. with Zaslow, J. (2010). *The Last Lecture* (London: Two Roads).

Peters, S. (2012). *The Chimp Paradox: The Mind Management Programme for Confidence, Success and Happiness* (London: Random House).

Robbins, A. (1992). *Awaken the Giant Within: How to Take Immediate Control of Your Mental, Emotional, Physical and Financial Life* (New York: Pocket Books).

Rubin, G. (2015). *Better Than Before: Mastering the Habits of Our Everyday Lives* (London: Two Roads).

Syed, M. (2011). *Bounce: The Myth of Talent and the Power of Practice* (London: 4th Estate).

Tough, P. (2013). *How Children Succeed: Grit, Curiosity and the Hidden Power of Character* (London: Random House).

Tracy, B. (2013). *Eat That Frog! Get More of the Important Things Done – Today!* (London: Hodder).

www.crownhouse.co.uk

ISBN 978-178583415-8

9 781785 834158

Education   Further Education Study Guide